Tobacco in Co

Virginia

"The Sovereign Remedy"

G. Melvin Herndon

Alpha Editions

This edition published in 2023

ISBN : 9789362095176

Design and Setting By
Alpha Editions
www.alphaedis.com
Email - info@alphaedis.com

TOBACCO IN COLONIAL VIRGINIA

"The Sovereign Remedy"

Tobacco was probably first brought to the shores of England from Florida by Sir John Hawkins in 1565. Englishmen were growing it by the 1570's, and after the return of the daring Sir Francis Drake to England with a large quantity of tobacco captured in the West Indies in 1586, the use of tobacco in England was increased substantially. By 1604 its consumption had become so extensive as to lead to the publication of King James' *Counter Blast*, condemning the use of tobacco; nevertheless, six years later the amount brought into Great Britain was valued at £60,000.

Some of the colonists were probably acquainted with tobacco before they landed at Jamestown and found the Indians cultivating and using it under the name of uppowoc or apooke. However, it was not until 1612 that its cultivation began among the English settlers, even in small patches. Previously their attention had been centered entirely on products that could be used for food. Captain John Smith wrote that none of the native crops were planted at first, not even tobacco.

The story of tobacco in Virginia begins with the ingenious John Rolfe. He was one of the many Englishmen who had come to enjoy the fragrant aroma and taste of the imported Spanish tobacco; and upon his arrival at Jamestown in May, 1610, Rolfe found that tobacco could be obtained only by buying it from the Indians, or by cultivating it. There seems to have been no spontaneous growth then as now. Owing to the frequent unfriendly atmosphere between the colonists and the Indians, Rolfe probably decided to grow a small patch for his own use. He also had a desire to find some profitable commodity that could be sold in England and thus promote the success and prosperity of the settlers and the London Company. Driven by these two motives John Rolfe became the first colonist to successfully grow tobacco, the plant that was to wield such a tremendous influence on the history of Virginia.

Nicotiana rustica, the native tobacco of North America, was found to be inferior to that grown in the Spanish Colonies. Botanists state that *Nicotiana rustica* had a much greater nicotine content and sprouted or branched more than that cultivated today. William Strachey, one of the first colonists, gave the following description of the native plant grown in 1616:

It is not of the best kynd, it is but poore and weake, and of a byting tast, it growes not fully a yard above the ground, bearing a little yellowe flower, like to hennebane, the leaves are short and thick, somewhat round at the upper end....

In 1611 Rolfe decided to experiment with seed of the mild Spanish variety. He persuaded a shipmaster to bring him some tobacco seed from the Island of Trinidad and Caracas, Venezuela; and by June, 1612, tobacco from the imported seeds was being cultivated at Jamestown. On July 20, 1613, a Captain Robert Adams landed the *Elizabeth* in England with a sample of Rolfe's first experimental crop. In England, this first shipment was described as excellent in quality, but it was still inferior to Spanish tobacco. In 1616 Rolfe modestly asserted, "no doubt but after a little more triall and expense in the curing thereof, it will compare with the best in the West Indies." The success of Rolfe's experiment was soon apparent. In 1617, 20,000 pounds of tobacco were exported from Virginia, and in the following year the amount doubled.

Tobacco did not become the chief staple owing merely to the successful attempts by Rolfe to produce a satisfactory smoking leaf. As has been noted, there was a ready market for tobacco in England before the settlers landed at Jamestown. A second important cause was the fact that tobacco was indigenous to the soil and climate of Virginia. Tobacco also had a greater advantage Over All Other Staples in That It Could Be Produced in Larger Quantities Per Acre. This Was Important Considering the Labor Required To Clear the Trees and Prepare One Acre for Cultivation. It Was Soon Discovered That the Amount of Tobacco Produced by One Man's Labor Was Worth About Six Times the Amount of Wheat That One Man Could Grow and Harvest. Moreover, Tobacco Could Be Shipped More Economically Than Any Other Crop; Thus the Monetary Return Upon a Cargo Was Greater Than for Any Other Crop That Could Be Produced in the Colony.

One Other Factor Must Not Be Overlooked. One of the Basic Aims of the English Colonial Policy Was the Development Of Colonial Resources, Which Would at the Same Time Create a Colonial Market for English Manufactures in the Colonies. Tobacco Proved To Be Virginia's Most Valuable Staple, and With Everyone Feverishly Growing the Plant, the Colony Became an Important Colonial Market. Virginia Purchased English Goods Delivered in English Ships With Her Tobacco, England Marketed Much of the Tobacco In Europe and Received Specie Or Goods That Could Be Sold Elsewhere. This Created a Market for English Manufactures, the English Merchant Fleet Profited From the Carrying Trade and There Was No Drain of Specie From England.

THE TOBACCO PLANTATION: FROM JAMESTOWN TO THE BLUE RIDGE

The cultivation of tobacco soon spread from John Rolfe's garden to every available plot of ground within the fortified districts in Jamestown. By 1617 the value of tobacco was well known in every settlement or plantation in Virginia—Bermuda, Dale's Gift, Henrico, Jamestown, Kecoughtan, and West and Shirley Hundreds—each under a commander. Governor Dale allowed its culture to be gradually extended until it absorbed the whole attention at West and Shirley Hundreds and Jamestown.

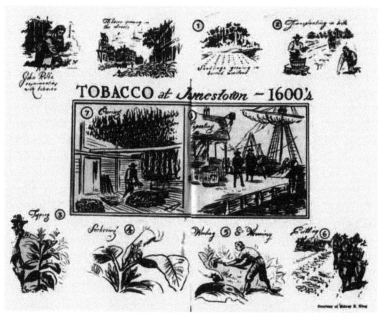

TOBACCO at Jamestown—1600's
Courtesy of Sidney E. King

The first general planting in the colony began at West and Shirley Hundreds where twenty-five men, commanded by a Captain Madison, were employed solely in planting and curing tobacco. In 1616 the tobacco fever struck furiously in Jamestown. The following description indicates the impact of the "fever": there were "but five or six houses, the church downe, the palizado's broken, the bridge in pieces, the well of fresh water spoiled; the storehouse used for the church..., [and] the colony dispersed all about, planting tobacco." The "Noxious weed" was even growing in the streets and in the market place.

By 1622 plantations extended at intervals from Point Comfort as far as 140 miles up the James River, and the planters were so absorbed in the cultivation of tobacco that they gave the Indians firearms and employed them to do their hunting. This boldness was shortlived, for the Indian Massacre of 1622 tended to narrow the area under cultivation for that year. Even so, the planters were able to produce 60,000 pounds of tobacco.

Within a year after the massacre the settlers once again became very bold and extended cultivated areas even farther than before. Prior to the massacre, the planters had difficulty in clearing the ground of timber; afterwards, they took over the fields cleared by the Indians which were said to be among the best in the colony. Expansion was further facilitated by the "head-right" system, introduced in 1618, which gave fifty acres of land to any person who transported a settler to the colony.

For the first twenty years after the landing at Jamestown, the settlers restricted themselves to the valley of the James and to the Accomac Peninsula. For the next thirty years there was a gradual expansion to the north and west along the banks of the James, York, and the Rappahannock rivers and their tributaries. By 1650 the frontiersmen had reached the Potomac. From Jamestown, settlements gradually spread up and down both banks of the James and its tributaries, the Elizabeth, Nansemond, Appomattox, and the Chickahominy. Then came the settlements along the York and its tributaries, the Mattapony and the Pamunkey; and finally, along the banks of the Rappahannock and the Potomac. The expansion into the interior did not take place until the Tidewater area had become fairly well settled. The tidal creeks and rivers afforded a safe and convenient means of communication while the country was thickly forested and infested with unfriendly Indians. By settling on the peninsulas, formed by the tidal creeks and rivers, it was easier to protect the early settlements once the Indians had been driven out.

In 1629 there were from 4,000 to 5,000 English settlers, confined almost exclusively to the James River valley and to the Accomac Peninsula, where they cultivated about 2,000 acres of tobacco. By 1635 tobacco had almost disappeared in the immediate vicinity of Jamestown, as many of the planters moved to new land along the south bank of the York River. At this time there were settlements in the following eight counties: Henrico, located on both sides of the James River, between Arrahattock and Shirley Hundred; Charles City, also located on both sides of the James from Shirley Hundred Island to Weyanoke; James City, on both sides of the James from Chippoakes to Lawnes Creek, and from the Chickahominy River on the north side to a point nearly opposite the mouth of Lawnes Creek; Warrasquoke (Isle of Wight), contained the area from the southern limit of James City to the Warrasquoke River; Warwick and Elizabeth City, the rest of the remaining settlements on the James River; Charles River (York), all of the plantations on the south bank of the York River; and finally Accomac. The plantations were still more thickly grouped in James City than in any other county.

By the late 1630's, attempts to reduce the amount of tobacco grown in the colony, by limiting the number of plants each person could plant, had caused many planters to leave their plantations in search of virgin soil in which more tobacco per plant could be grown. They frequently built temporary dwellings, as they expected to move on as soon as the land under cultivation showed signs of exhaustion. In 1648 planters in large numbers sought permission from Governor Berkeley and the Council to move across the York River, to take up the virgin and unclaimed land.

Spreading north the frontiersmen had reached the Rappahannock and the Potomac by 1650, and settlers began moving into Lancaster County. In 1653 the first settlers established themselves in what is now King William County. Just before the end of the seventeenth century the tobacco industry had expanded into the lowlands all along the Rappahannock and Potomac rivers below the Fall Line. In 1689 the York River area produced the largest quantity of tobacco, the Rappahannock River area was second, the Upper James third, and the Accomac Peninsula last. While the production of tobacco continued to expand north and west, it made little headway in the sandy counties of Princess Anne and Norfolk.

All during the seventeenth century expansion tended to extend in a northerly direction within the Tidewater region, but in the eighteenth century the movement was to the west in search of virgin soil. Planters began moving beyond the Fall Line soon after the turn of the century. Robert Carter of Nomini Hall patented over 900 acres of land above the Falls in 1707. It is generally agreed that the commercial production of tobacco began to expand beyond the Fall Line about 1720. In 1723 a traveler, who had just visited above the Falls, mentioned seeing many fields of tobacco. In the following year Robert Carter had hundreds of additional acres surveyed, in what is now Prince William County, as he extended his holdings above the Fall Line. The tobacco industry seems to have been fairly well established as far west as Spotsylvania, Hanover, and Goochland counties as early as 1730.

In the year 1740 Elias and William Edmunds were among the first settlers in Fauquier County. They settled near what is now Warrenton and began producing tobacco of excellent quality, which soon came to be known as "Edmonium Tobacco." Ten years later large quantities were being produced in Albemarle (including present Nelson and Amherst counties), Cumberland,

Augusta, and Culpeper counties. During the six-year period 1750-1755, tobacco production appears to have been centered equally in three areas: the Upper James River district, the York River district, and the Rappahannock River district. Each of the three districts exported about 83,000 hogsheads of tobacco, while the Lower James River district exported only about 10,000.

Just prior to the American Revolution the tobacco industry began to expand rapidly south of the James River, especially to the south and west of Petersburg. One observer declared in 1769 that the Petersburg warehouses contained more tobacco than all the rest of the warehouses on the James or the York River. It was estimated that 20,000 hogsheads were being produced annually in that region alone. A considerable amount of tobacco was also being grown in the lower region of the Valley of Virginia.

As the tobacco industry continued to expand into Piedmont Virginia, there was a gradual decline in the Tidewater area. The increase in population naturally caused a continual expansion of the tobacco industry from its meager beginnings at Jamestown, but this was not the major cause. The primary cause was the wasteful cultivation methods practiced by the planters. To obtain the greatest yield from his land the planter raised three or four consecutive crops of tobacco in one field, then moved on to virgin fields. This practice was begun on a relatively large scale as early as 1632 when a planting restriction of 1,500 plants per person was enacted, causing many planters to leave their estates in search of better land in an effort to increase the quality of their tobacco. As cheap virgin soil became scarce, planters left their lands in Tidewater to take up fresh acreage in the Piedmont, or they stayed at home and grew grain, some corn but mostly wheat.

We can only generalize as to when and how extensive this substitution of wheat for tobacco may have been. There are those who believe that a permanent shift away from tobacco began as early as 1720 on the Eastern Shore of Virginia, while others state that it did not start until about ten years later. As early as 1759 all of the best lands in Virginia were reported to have been taken, and by the time of the Revolution the supply was said to have been completely exhausted. In 1771 there were rumors that at least one hundred of the principal Virginia planters had given up the tobacco culture entirely and converted their plantations to something more profitable. However, it is generally agreed that tobacco was not abandoned extensively in Tidewater before the Revolution.

The first appreciable decline came during the Revolution and this trend continued until the tobacco was almost completely abandoned in Tidewater in the nineteenth century. The rise in demand for foodstuffs during the war caused planters to shift from tobacco in increasing numbers. Many of them only reduced their tobacco crop at first, but later abandoned it completely.

After the Revolution wheat was substituted for tobacco quite extensively, but owing to the expansion into the Piedmont, Virginia's post-war tobacco production soon equalled that of the prewar years. Tobacco was still grown in Tidewater Virginia and some beyond the western boundary of the Piedmont, but by this time Tidewater had ceased to be the "tobacco country" of previous years.

The production of tobacco continued to increase in the Piedmont and decrease in Tidewater, and Piedmont Virginia became more firmly established as Virginia's tobacco belt. This change was due partly to the fact that the virgin and fertile soils of the West kept tobacco prices so low that it could not be profitably produced on the manured worn out soils in the East. Tidewater was becoming full of old tobacco fields covered with young pine trees and the industry became concentrated largely in middle and southern Virginia. By 1800 Piedmont Virginia had definitely become the major tobacco producing area.

Old Tobacco Warehouse, built 1680 at Urbanna, Virginia
Courtesy of Mrs. H. I. Worthington

The mild species of tobacco which Rolfe imported from the West Indies.

The harsh species of tobacco which Rolfe found the Indians cultivating.

Courtesy of George Arents, and Virginia State Library

Expansion and new developments over a period of years brought about a fantastic increase in tobacco production. When its production was confined to the Tidewater area, Virginia produced about 40,000,000 pounds annually; by 1800 this amount had doubled. Virginia remained the leading producer of tobacco in the United States until the War Between the States, when she was replaced by Kentucky, owing to the devastating effects of the war in the Old Dominion.

In the South the nature of the crop usually determines the number of acres that one person can cultivate successfully. Only a small number of acres of tobacco can be cultivated properly owing to its high value of yield per acre and the careful supervision required. The production of tobacco per acre does not appear to have changed very much in the long period from about 1650 to 1800, when 1,000 pounds per acre was considered a good yield. However, the amount that one man could produce increased during this period as the planters became more experienced and the plow and other implements came to be used more extensively. It has been estimated that in 1624 one man could properly cultivate and harvest only about one-half of an acre of tobacco, or about 400 pounds. At the beginning of the eighteenth century the average product of one man was from 1,500 to 2,000 pounds or in terms of acreage, from one and a half to two acres, plus six or seven barrels of corn. Around 1775 one man produced from 2,000 to 2,500 pounds of tobacco besides provisions. Thus it appears that during most of the Colonial period one man could cultivate one and a half to two acres of tobacco, plus provisions; but by the end of this period he had increased the productiveness of his own labor.

MANAGEMENT OF THE CROP

Cultivation practices during the early years at Jamestown appear to have been a combination of those used by the Indians and those of the farmers in England; modifications and new techniques were developed as the settlers became experienced planters. The early Jamestown settlers followed the Indian custom of planting the tobacco seed in hills as they did corn, although some probably followed the practice as described by Stevens and Liebault's *Maison Rustique* or *The Country Farm*, published in London in 1606:

For to sow it, you must make a hole in the earth with your finger and that as deep as your finger is long, then you must cast into the same hole ten or twelve seeds of the said Nicotiana together, and fill up the hole again: for it is so small, as that if you should put in but four or five seeds the earth would choake it: and if the time be dry, you must water the place easily some five days after: And when the herb is grown out of the earth, inasmuch as every seed will have put up his sprout and stalk, and that the small thready roots are entangled the one within the other, you must with a great knife make a compass within the earth in the places about this plot where they grow and take up the earth and all together, and cast them into a bucket full of water, to the end that the earth may be separated, and the small and tender impes swim about the water; and so you shall sunder them one after another without breaking them.

This was perhaps the forerunner of the tobacco plantbed, as it appears from the above description that a half dozen or so plants were taken from each hill sown and transplanted nearby.

Just when the planters stopped planting tobacco like corn is not known. Thomas Glover's *Account of Virginia*, written in 1671, is perhaps the first written account which mentions sowing the seeds in beds. He wrote, "In the Twelve-daies [before Christmas?] they begin to sow their seed in the beds of fine Mould..." A somewhat more detailed account was written in 1688 by John Clayton, an English clergyman visiting in Virginia. He relates that before the seeds were sown the planters tested the seed by throwing a few into the fire; if they sparkled like gunpowder, they were declared to be good. The ground was chopped fine and the seeds, mixed with ashes, were sown around the middle of January. To protect the young plants, the seedbed was usually covered with oak leaves, though straw was used occasionally. Straw was thought to harbor and breed a fly that destroyed the young plants, and if straw was used, it was first smoked with brimstone to kill this fly. Oak boughs were then placed on top of the leaves or straw and left there until the frosts were gone, at which time they were removed so that the young tender plants were exposed to allow them to grow strong and large enough to be transplanted.

Post-Revolutionary plantbed practices were essentially those of the early colonial planters, with slight modifications as they became more experienced. In choosing plantbed sites, a sunny southern or southeastern exposure on a virgin slope near a stream was preferred. This enabled the planter to water his plantbed in case of a drought. The practice of burning the plantbeds over with piles of brush and logs prior to seeding was no doubt a seventeenth century custom, but the first available record was found in an account written during the Revolution.

To clear land for cultivation, the settlers felled the trees about a yard from the ground to prevent the stump from sprouting and to cause the stump to decay sooner. Some of the wood was burnt or carried off and the rest was left on the field to rot. The area between the stumps and logs was then broken up with the hoe. In their ardent quest for more cleared land, the planters frequently cultivated old Indian fields, which the Indian had abandoned for one reason or another. Such land was always found to be of the best soil. Clayton stated that after the land was chopped fine, hills to set every plant in were raised to "about the bigness of a common Mole-hill...." A later account by William Tatham, relates that the hills were made by drawing a round heap of earth about knee high around the leg of the worker, the foot was then withdrawn and the top of the hill was flattened with the back of the hoe.

In 1628 the hills were made at a distance of four and one-half feet, the distance was reduced to four feet by 1671, and by 1700, three feet became and remained the usual distance. The plants were considered large enough to be transplanted when they had grown to be about the "Breadth of a Shilling," usually around the first or second week in May. The earlier in May the better, so that the crop would mature in time to harvest before the frosts came. Planters usually waited for a rain or "season" to begin transplanting. One person with a container (usually a basket) of plants dropped a plant near each hill; another followed, made a hole in the center of each hill with his fingers, inserted the roots and pressed the earth around the roots with his hands. Several "seasons" and several drawings from the plantbeds were usually required before the entire crop was planted, which was frequently not until sometime in July.

The tobacco was hoed for the first time about eight to ten days after planting, or to use a common expression, when the plants had "taken root." The tobacco was usually hoed once each week or as often as was deemed necessary to keep the soil "loose" and the weeds down. When the plants were about knee high they were "hilled up," as the Indian had done his corn, or the Englishman his cabbage, and considered "laid by." Frequently some of the plants died or were cut off by an earthworm; these vacant hills were usually replanted during the month of June, except when prohibited by law. This restriction was an attempt to reduce the amount of inferior tobacco at harvest time.

Around 1800, plows were still rarely used in new grounds, but they appear to have been rather common in the old fields. George Washington used the plow to lay off his tobacco rows into three-foot squares, the hills were then made directly on the cross so that in the early stages of its growth the tobacco could be cultivated with the plow each way. The plow lightened the burden of cultivation by requiring less hoe work.

When the plant began to bloom, usually six or seven weeks after planting, the plant was topped; that is, the top of the plant was pinched out with the thumb and finger nails. The number of leaves left on the plant depended largely upon the fertility of the soil. In the early days of the colony, planters left twenty-five or thirty leaves on a plant, by 1671 the number had been reduced to twelve or sixteen in very rich soil. Throughout the seventeenth century the General Assembly, in an attempt to reduce production, occasionally limited the number of leaves that could be left on a plant after topping. After around 1700, from five to nine leaves were left on the plant, depending on the strength of the soil.

After topping, the plant grew no higher, but the leaves grew larger and heavier and sprouts or suckers appeared at the junction of the stalk and the leaf stem. If allowed to grow they injured the marketable quality of tobacco by taking up plant food that would have gone into the leaves. These suckers were removed by pinching them off with the thumb and finger nails. Owing to his laziness or ignorance, the Indian did not top his tobacco, though he did keep the suckers out. Tobacco that has been topped will produce a second set of suckers once the first growth has been removed. If the tobacco is not topped, only three or four suckers will appear, and these grow in the very top of the plant. During the course of the growing season the colonial planter had two sets of suckers to remove, from the junction of each leaf and from the bottom to the top of the plant, whereas the Indian had only a total of three or four per plant. Thus it appears that the planter learned from his own experience to top tobacco, and that it was a laborious though profitable task. It has been said that topping was first used as a means of limiting the production of tobacco to the very best grades by the planters as early as the 1620's.

Only a planter with considerable experience could tell when the plant was ripe for harvest. This no doubt accounts for much of the inferior tobacco produced in the early days of the colony. Planters usually had their own individual methods of determining when a plant was ripe for cutting. Some thought the plants were ripe and ready to cut when a vigorous growth of suckers appeared around the root; others believed the plant was ripe when the top leaves of the plant became covered with yellow spots and "rolled over," touching the ground. Occasionally it had to be cut regardless of its maturity to save it from the frost.

During the early days at Jamestown the tobacco was harvested by pulling the ripe leaves from the plants growing in the fields. The leaves were then piled in heaps and covered with hay to be cured by sweating. In 1617, a Mr. Lambert discovered that the leaves cured better when strung on lines than when sweated under the hay. This innovation was further facilitated in 1618 when Governor Argall prohibited the use of hay to sweat tobacco, owing to the scarcity of fodder for the cattle. It was probably this new method of curing that led to the building of tobacco barns, which were known to be in use at the time of the Indian Massacre in 1622.

By 1671 the planters had stopped stringing the leaves on lines; the tobacco plant was cut off just above the top of the ground and left lying in the field for three or four hours, or until the leaves "fell" or became somewhat withered so that the plant could be handled without breaking the stems and fibers in the leaves. The plants were then carried into the tobacco barns, and hung on tobacco sticks by a small peg that had been driven into each stalk.

During the early years of the eighteenth century the pegs were superseded by partially spliting the stalk and hanging it on the sticks. The use of fire in curing tobacco was also introduced during this century, but was rarely used before the Revolution. The earlier accounts refer to curing as the action of the air and sun. If the plant was large, the stalk was split down the middle six or seven inches below the extremity of the split, then turned directly bottom upwards to enable the sun to cause it to "fall", or wither faster. The plants were then brought to the scaffolds, which were generally erected all around the tobacco barns, and placed with the splits across a small oak stick about an inch in diameter and four and a half feet long. The sticks of tobacco were then placed on the scaffold. The tobacco remained there to cure for a brief period and then the sticks were removed from the outdoor scaffolds, carried into the tobacco barn and placed on the tier poles erected in successive regular graduation from near the bottom to the top of the barn. Once the barn was filled, the curing was sometimes hastened by making fires on the floor of the barn.

Around 1800 the most common method was still air-curing, fire was used primarily to keep the tobacco from molding in damp weather. During the War of 1812 there was a considerable shift to fire-curing owing to the demand in Europe for a smoky flavored leaf. Fire-curing not only gave tobacco a different taste, but it also improved the keeping qualities of the leaf. The fire dried the stem of the leaf more thoroughly, thus eliminating the major cause of spoilage when packed in the hogshead for shipment.

August and September were the favorite months for cutting and curing because the tobacco would cure a brighter color if cured in hot weather. Even today farmers like to finish curing their tobacco as early in September as possible. However, it was usually cold weather before all of the crop could be cut and cured. Occasionally frost would kill part of the crop before it was ripe enough to cut.

In the early years of the tobacco industry there was little to the stripping process as the leaves were hung on strings to cure. The string was removed and the leaves were twisted and wound into rolls. The leaves were twisted by hand or spun on a small spinning machine into a thick rope, from which a ball containing from one to thirty pounds was made, though some were known to weigh as much as 105 pounds. The rolls were either wrapped in heavy canvass or packed in small barrels for shipping. In 1614 four barrels containing 170 pounds each were sent to England on the *Sir Thomas*. Tobacco was also shipped loose or in small bundles known as hands, and by 1629 a considerable number of hogsheads were being used.

There seems to have been little grading in the early days. London Company officials frequently complained of the bad tobacco being mixed with the good, and early inspection laws required that the tobacco be brought to central locations and the mean tobacco separated from the bulk. After cutting became the common practice the leaves were stripped from the stalk and assorted according to variety and grade. By the 1680's the lowest grade was known as lugs. Sweet-scented and Oronoco were usually exported separately, and usually only the sweet-scented was stemmed. If the two varieties were mixed in a hogshead, it was purchased at the prevailing Oronoco prices, which were less than those paid for sweet-scented. The English merchant claimed that he had to sell all of it as Oronoco unless it were separated and that the cost of the labor required to separate it was equal to the higher price the sweet-scented would bring. These two varieties were probably seldom mixed except perhaps to fill the last hogshead of the season. The planters eventually came to realize the value of handling tobacco with care, for when good tobacco land became less plentiful, other means of improving the quality of tobacco became necessary.

By 1665 most of the tobacco was shipped in hogsheads, but it was not until 1730 that the shipment of bulk tobacco was prohibited. Nor were the hogsheads made to any standard size until 1657, at which time they were required to be 43" × 26". In 1695 the standard size was raised to 48" × 30", and this remained the standard size until the 1790's. In 1796 the legal size was increased to 54" × 34"; this remained the legal size until the 1820's. The weight of the hogshead increased from time to time. In 1657 a hogshead of tobacco weighed about 300 pounds, 600 in the 1660's, 800 by 1730, 950 by 1765, and around 1,000 in the 1790's. These were supposed to have been the standard or legal weights, but regulations were not strictly enforced. As early as 1757 some of the hogsheads weighed as much as 1,274 pounds. By 1800 hogsheads averaged about 1,100 pounds.

VARIETIES

A complete story on the origin of the early varieties of tobacco would be a very significant contribution, since very little is known about them. Most writers agree that the tobacco cultivated by the English settlers was not the same *Nicotiana rustica* grown by the Indians, but *Nicotiana tabacum*, the type found growing in South America and the West Indies. The difference between these two types was profound, both in taste and size. The plant native to Virginia was small, growing to a height of only two or three feet, whereas *Nicotiana tabacum* grew from six to nine feet tall. As to taste, George Arents remarked, "the same difference in taste exists between these two species, as between a crab apple and an Albemarle pippin."

All during the colonial period tobacco was classified into two main varieties, Oronoco and sweet-scented. Oronoco had a large porous pointed leaf and was strong in taste. Sweet-scented was milder, the leaf was rounder and the fibers were finer. We are also told that sweet-scented grew mostly in the lower parts of Virginia, along the York and James rivers, and later on the Rappahannock and on the southside of the Potomac. Oronoco was generally planted up the Chesapeake Bay area and in the back settlements on the strong land along all the rivers.

Oronoco is thought to have originated in the vicinity of the Orinoco River valley in Venezuela. After being brought to a different environment and climate in Virginia, various varieties or strains of Oronoco were developed or came about naturally. In the late 1600's a very fair and bright large Oronoco, Prior, and Kite's Foot were mentioned. As the years passed planters came to distinguish other varieties such as Hudson, Frederick, Thick-Joint, Shoe-string, Thickset, Blue Pryor, Medley Pryor, White Stem, Townsend, Long Green, Little Frederic, and Browne Oronoco.

A type of tobacco referred to locally as "yellow", had been growing on the poor, thin, and sandy soils in and around Pittsylvania County, Virginia, and Caswell County, North Carolina since the early 1820's. It was just another one of the many local varieties and attracted little attention until a very lucky accident occurred in 1839. A Negro slave on the Slade farm in Caswell County, North Carolina, fell asleep while fire-curing tobacco. Upon awakening, he quickly piled some dry wood on the dying embers; the sudden drying heat from the revived fires produced a profound effect—this particular barn of tobacco cured a bright yellow. This accident produced a curing technique that soon became known throughout the surrounding area in Virginia and North Carolina. This tobacco became known as "Bright-Tobacco", and this area the "Bright-Tobacco Belt".

The many variations were due to the different environments, cultural practices, methods of curing and breeding; and each of these variations was given a name because of some particular quality it possessed, or was given the name of a person or place. The difference in the composition of the "Bright-Tobacco" grown in the poor sandy soil, such as that found in Pittsylvania County, caused the tobacco to cure bright. This so called new type of tobacco was of the old Virginia Oronoco and if grown on heavier soils, it produced a much heavier bodied tobacco and would not make the same response when flue-cured. Only the tobacco grown in the soils such as that in the "Bright-Tobacco Belt" cured bright, which indicates that it was the soil and not the variety that caused the tobacco to be bright when cured.

The origin and development of sweet-scented tobacco remains somewhat of a mystery, and we can only make conjectures as to what happened. Some authorities hold that the present day Maryland tobacco is descended from the sweet-scented of the Colonial days, while others believe it to be a descendant of Oronoco. It seems quite possible that there was only one variety of *Nicotiana tabacum* when John Rolfe first began his experiments, and there is reason to believe that this first tobacco was sweet-scented. The name Oronoco probably came after the name sweet-scented had already been established. It also appears that sweet-scented disappeared as soon as the soils along the James, York, Rappahannock, and Potomac rivers were exhausted.

George Arents, probably the foremost authority on the history of tobacco, in referring to Rolfe's first shipment to England wrote, "So fragrant was the leaf that it almost at once began to be known as 'sweet-scented.'" Ralph Hamor, in 1614, declared that the colony grew tobacco equal to that of Trinidad, "sweet and pleasant." Jerome E. Brooks wrote that Rolfe's importation of tobacco seed resulted in the famous Virginia sweet-scented leaf.

Once the cultivation began to spread into the areas away from the sandy loam along the James and York rivers, the type of soil necessary for the production of the sweet-scented, other varieties began to develop. In 1688 John Clayton wrote, "I have observed, that that which is called Pine-wood Land tho' it be a sandy soil, even the sweet-scented Tobacco that grows thereon, is large and porous, agreeable to Aranoko Tobacco; it smokes as coursely as Aranoko." While on his visit to Virginia, Clayton visited a poor, worn-out plantation along the James River. The owner, a widow, complained to him that her land would produce only four or five leaves of tobacco per plant. Clayton suggested that one of the bogs on the plantation be drained and planted in tobacco. A few years later Clayton happened to meet this same lady in London, selling the first crop of tobacco grown on the drained bog. She related to Clayton that the product was "so very large, that it was suspected to be of the Aranoko kind...."

In 1724 Hugh Jones observed that the farther a person went northward from the York or southward from the James, the poorer the quality of the sweet-scented tobacco, "but this maybe (I believe) attributed in some Measure to the Seed and Management, as well as to the Land and Latitude." John Custis in a letter to Philip Perry in 1737 wrote that he grew Oronoco on the Eastern Shore of Virginia using the same seed as he did for his sweet-scented York crop. It appears that as the sandy loam necessary for the growing of sweet-scented tobacco became exhausted and the planters expanded into the heavy fertile soils, the tobacco became the strong, coarse Oronoco. As virgin soil became scarce, Oronoco was no longer confined to the richest soils, nor was it thought to be less sweet-scented than its rivals. Toward the end of the eighteenth century tobacco inspectors found it so difficult to distinguish the various types, that they classed all tobacco as Oronoco. Thus it seems quite possible that both Oronoco and sweet-scented were originally one variety which became two, primarily because of the different soil composition.

TRANSPORTATION TO MARKET

In the early days of the colony the small ocean-going merchant vessel was the only method of transportation essential to marketing the tobacco crop. Such a small ship was able to anchor at many of the plantation wharves and load its cargo of tobacco. Next to fertility, the proximity to navigable water was the most important factor in influencing the planter in the selection of a tract of land. However, later expansion of the tobacco industry into the interior and the increase in the size of all ocean-going ships made some mode of transportation within the colony a necessity. When the ships could not get directly up to the wharf or enter shallow creeks on which many of the plantations were located, small boats called flats or shallops were used to transport the hogsheads to the anchored vessels. In 1633 the General Assembly provided that all tobacco had to be brought to one of the five warehouses—to be erected in specified localities—to be stored until sold. The planters objected immediately and petitioned the House of Burgesses to allow ships to come into every county, "where they will find at every man's house a store convenient enough for theire ladinge, we beinge all seated by the Riverside." The planters also complained that they had "... noe other means to export but by Boatinge."

Carrying the tobacco for long distances in the shallop involved a risk, as well as an additional expense. By rolling the hogsheads directly on board a ship anchored at his own wharf or only a few miles away the planter eliminated the danger involved in transporting his tobacco in an untrustworthy, heavily laden shallop, and he also saved the increase in freight charges for delivery to the ships by the seamen. Freight rates were the same from his wharf to England as they were from any other point in the colony.

In 1697 Henry Hartwell remarked, "they [the merchants] are at the charge of carting this tobacco ... [collected from the planter,] to convenient Landinge; or if it lyes not far from these landings, they must trust to the Seamen for their careful rolling it on board of their sloops and shallops...." A second common mode of transportation, according to Philip A. Bruce, was "not to draw the cask over the ground by means of horses or oxen, like an enormous clod crusher, the custom of a later period, but to propel it by the application of a steady force from behind." In 1724 Hugh Jones wrote, "The tobacco is rolled, drawn by horses, or carted to convenient Rolling Houses, whence it is conveyed on board the ships in flats or sloops." Thus it appears that by 1700 the Tidewater planters had adopted three methods of transporting their tobacco to market or to points of exportation: by rolling the hogshead, by cart, and by boat.

By the middle of the eighteenth century planters in the Piedmont were rolling their tobacco to the distant Tidewater markets, whereas the Tidewater planter usually hauled his tobacco by wagon. Rolling tobacco more than 100 miles was not out of the ordinary. The ingenious upland planters placed some extra hickory hoops around the hogshead, attached two hickory limbs for shafts, by driving pegs into the headings, and hitched a horse or oxen to it. This method worked quite well except that the tobacco was frequently damaged by the mud, water, or sand. To prevent this, the hogshead was raised off the ground by a device called a felly. This device consisted of segments of wood fitted together to form a circle resembling the rim of a cartwheel; these segments were fitted around the circumference of the hogshead. The hogsheads used for rolling in this manner were constructed much more substantially than those wagoned or transported by boat.

For the river trade the Piedmont planter once again relied upon his ingenuity. Around 1740 a rather unique water carrier was perfected by the Reverend Robert Rose, then living in Albemarle County. Two canoes fifty or sixty feet long were lashed together with cords and eight or nine hogsheads of tobacco were rolled on their gunwales crossways for the trip to Richmond. This came to be known as the "Rose method." For the return trip the canoes were separated and two men with poles could travel twice the distance in a day as four good oarsmen could propel a boat capable of carrying the same burden. Before 1795 boats coming down the James River from the back country landed at Westham, located just above the falls, and the tobacco was then carried into Richmond by wagon. There is the story of one planter who forgot to land his canoes at Westham. It seems that he left his plantation on the upper James with a load of tobacco and a jug full of whiskey. By the time he reached Westham the planter had consumed too much of the whiskey, and forgot to land at Westham. He rode his canoes, tobacco and all, over the Falls. Shortly thereafter he was fished from the waters downstream, wet and frightened, but sober.

By 1800, owing to the fact that both the planters and buyers had become more concerned about the quality of tobacco, rolling tobacco in hogsheads began to decline sharply, although fifty years later a rare roller might still be seen on his way to market. The rivers and canals provided the most typical means of transportation. Wagons were used primarily as feeders to and from inland waters. The Potomac, Rappahannock, and York rivers were valuable colonial arteries, but played a less significant role after the Piedmont became the major producing area. The James and the Roanoke superseded them as the major arteries of transportation in the nineteenth century.

The "Rose method" of water transportation, the lashing of two canoes together, had practically disappeared on the upland waters by 1800, being replaced by a small open flat-bottomed boat called the bateau, which carried a load of from five to eight hogsheads. Two planters, N. C. Dawson and A. Rucker, both of Amherst County, patented a bateau, in the early 1800's, which was a great improvement over the earlier ones. This bateau was from forty-eight to fifty-four feet long, but very narrow in proportion to its length. It was claimed that with a crew of three men these new "James River Bateaux" could make the round trip from Lynchburg to Richmond in ten days. They floated down the stream with ease, but worked their way back upstream with poles. Shortly before the turn of the eighteenth century canals had been constructed around the falls from Westham to Richmond, and the upland boats were able to load and unload their cargoes at the wharves in Richmond. In 1810 it was estimated that about one-fourth of the entire Virginia tobacco crop came down the James River and through the Westham Canal into Richmond.

There were land and water routes in the Roanoke Valley that led to Petersburg. Tobacco was taken all the way to Petersburg by wagon, or carried by boat from the upper Roanoke and its tributaries to the falls at Weldon, North Carolina, and from there to Petersburg by wagon. Owing to the tobacco trade coming down the Roanoke, Clarksville became a small market town. In the Farmville area many of the planters sent their tobacco down the Appomattox River to Petersburg, rather than overland by wagon. Soon after 1800 the Upper Canal Company built a canal that connected Petersburg with the navigable waters of the Appomattox River. Virginia's waterways served her transportation problem well until they were superseded by the railroads in the ante-bellum days.

ORIGIN AND DEVELOPMENT OF THE INSPECTION SYSTEM

Within a few years after Rolfe's successful experiment in the cultivation of tobacco, it became necessary to inaugurate some means of improving the quality of the Virginia tobacco. Once it was discovered that tobacco could be successfully and profitably grown in Virginia, everyone wanted to grow it. Blacksmiths, carpenters, shipwrights, and even the minister frequently grew a patch of tobacco. Owing to inexperience in farming of any kind, plus the fact that the commercial production of tobacco was new even to most of the experienced farmers, much of the tobacco produced was of a very low quality. For centuries many planters seem to have placed quantity above quality in growing tobacco. Anyone could grow tobacco in certain quantities, but only a few could produce tobacco of superior quality.

The first general inspection law in Virginia was passed in 1619 and provided that all tobacco offered for exchange at the magazine, the general storehouse in Jamestown, found to be very "mean" in quality by the magazine custodian was to be burnt. The magazine was abolished in 1620 and in 1623 this law was amended to provide for the appointment of sworn men in each settlement to condemn all bad tobacco.

In 1630 an act was passed prohibiting the sale or acceptance of inferior tobacco in payment of debts. The commander of each plantation or settlement was authorized to appoint two or three experienced and competent men to help him inspect all tobacco, offered in payment of debts, which had been found "mean" by the creditor. If the inspectors declared the tobacco mean, the inferior tobacco was burned and the delinquent planter was disbarred from planting tobacco. Only the General Assembly could remove this disability. Owing to complaints that the commanders were showing partiality to planters on their own plantations, the act was amended in 1632; the commander's power of inspection was removed and his duty was limited to appointing two inspectors and making the final report. The appointment of inspectors was made compulsory in case of a complaint.

The following year (1633) a more comprehensive measure was enacted. It provided that all inspections were to be made at five different points in the colony: James City, Shirley Hundred Island, Denbigh, Southampton River in Elizabeth City, and Cheskiack. Storehouses were to be built at these places and all tobacco was to be brought to these storehouses before the last day of December of each year. At these storehouses the tobacco was to be carefully inspected and all of the bad tobacco separated from the good and burned. This duty was to be performed once each week by inspectors under oath, one of whom was to be a member of the Council. All tobacco found in the barns of the planters after December 31 was to be confiscated, unless reserved for family use. All of those planning to keep tobacco for that purpose were required to swear to this fact before the proper officials before December 31. All debts were to be paid at one of these five storehouses, with the storekeeper as a witness. Before the end of the year (1633) two other such storehouses were authorized to be built,—one at Warrasquoke and the other at a point lying between Weyanoke and the Falls. In addition to the Councillors, members of the local courts were added as inspectors. The provision requiring the burning of unmerchantable tobacco may have been enforced, but the storehouses were never built.

In 1639 all of the mean tobacco and half of the good was ordered destroyed. The legislature passed an act providing for the appointment of 213 inspectors, three were assigned to each district. These inspectors were authorized to break down the doors of any building if they had reason to believe that tobacco was being concealed within. This act was designed primarily to restrict the quantity of tobacco to be marketed owing to the flooded markets abroad and the resulting low prices.

All of the inspection laws passed after 1632 were formally repealed in 1641. The only important inspection law left on the statute books was the one passed in 1630 requiring the plantation commander, who was later replaced by the county lieutenant, to appoint two or three inspectors to inspect tobacco sold or received in payment of a debt, upon complaint of the buyer or creditor that he had been passed some bad tobacco. The law remained on the books until 1730. After these early attempts to establish an effective inspection system, little further progress was made during the seventeenth century. Occasional acts aimed at controlling the quantity and quality of tobacco continued to be passed from time to time; such as laws prohibiting the tending of seconds, false packing, and planting or replanting tobacco after a certain date.

As the tobacco industry continued to expand into the interior, the need and the difficulty of regulating the quality of the leaf increased. Owing to ignorance or indifference, the frontier planters seldom resorted to methods of improving the quality of the crop. They traded their tobacco in small lots with the outport merchants, those from ports other than London, mostly Scottish, who sold the inferior tobacco to the countries in northern Europe. In 1705 the Council proposed that an experienced and competent person be appointed in each county to inspect and receive all tobacco for discharge of debts in that county at specifically named storehouses and "at no other place." These county agents were to meet and select proper locations for building the storehouses. Owners of the land sites selected were to be given the privilege of building and renting these storehouses. If the owner did not choose to build, he could rent the land site to the county agent that he might build on it. If both refused to build, it was proposed that the county court should buy the land and erect the storehouse.

Storehouses were already established on many of the land sites proposed. In 1680, to accelerate the growth of towns, the General Assembly had passed an act providing that fifty acres of land be laid out for towns at convenient landings and that storehouses be built in each, at which all goods imported had to be landed and all exports stored while awaiting transportation. The towns and storehouses were located in the following places in twenty counties: Accomac, Calvert's Neck; Charles City, Flower de Hundred; Elizabeth City, Hampton; Gloucester, Tindall's Point; Henrico, Varina; Isle of Wight, Pates Field on Pagan Creek; James City, James City; Lancaster, Corotomond River; Middlesex, Urbanna Creek; Nansemond, Dues Point;

New Kent, Brick House; Norfolk, on the Elizabeth River at the mouth of the Eastern River; Northampton, Kings Creek; Northumberland, Chickacony; Essex, Hobb's Hole; Stafford, Pease Point, at the mouth of Deep Creek; Westmoreland, Nominie; and York, Ship Honors Store. Though none of the proposals were passed by the General Assembly in 1705, they were incorporated into later legislation and provided the basis for an effective inspection system.

In 1712 the General Assembly once again decided it would be advantageous to have designated places in each county where tobacco and other products could be kept safe while waiting for transportation to England, and an act was passed providing that all houses already built and being used as public "rolling-houses", that is warehouses, within one mile of a public landing, be maintained by their respective owners. If there were no such warehouses at designated locations, the county courts were given the authority to order new ones built. If the owner of the site refused to build, the county could, after a fair appraisal, buy the land and build a warehouse at public expense. When and if the warehouse was discontinued, the land reverted to the original owner or his heirs. It is interesting to know that the warehouse built at Urbanna, in Middlesex County, in 1680, is still standing, and it is "America's only colonial built warehouse for tobacco still in existence".

The owners were compelled to receive all goods offered, and were to receive storage rates for these services. For goods stored in casks of sixty gallons in size, or bales or parcels of greater bulk, the owners of the storehouses received twelve pence for the first day or the first three months and six pence for every three months thereafter. The owner of the warehouse was made liable for merchandise lost or damaged while under his custody.

One of the most significant features of the 1730 inspection system was first introduced in 1713. Primarily through the efforts of Governor Spotswood, an act was passed providing for licensed inspectors at the various warehouses already established. To provide a convenient circulating medium, and one that would not meet with opposition from the English government, these inspectors were authorized to issue negotiable receipts for tobacco inspected and stored at these warehouses. Like many new and untried ideas, this law seemed somewhat radical and met a great deal of opposition. With Colonel William Byrd as their leader, the opposition was able to convince certain British officials that the added expense required by the act imposed an undue hardship on the tobacco trade. This local opposition combined with the pressure of the conservative London merchants caused the act to be vetoed by the Privy Council in 1716.

The act of 1712, providing for the regulation of public warehouses, remained in force and became a part of the rather effective inspection system established in 1730. The act was amended in 1720 giving the county courts the authority to order warehouses inconvenient to the landings discontinued. These two pieces of legislation brought all of the public warehouses near convenient landings and made the warehouse movement flexible. From this point on, as the tobacco industry shifted from one area to another, the warehouse movement kept pace. From time to time established warehouses were ordered discontinued, or new ones erected; and occasionally warehouses ordered discontinued were revived. However, it appears that inspection warehouses were not permitted above the Fall Line until after the Revolution.

In 1730 the most comprehensive inspection bill ever introduced, passed the General Assembly. The common knowledge that the past and present inspection laws had failed to prevent the importation of unmarketable tobacco, plus a long depression, had changed the attitude of many of the influential planters and merchants. Nevertheless, the act did meet with opposition from some of the English customs officials and a few of the large planters. Soon after the passage of this new inspection law a prominent planter wrote complainingly to a London merchant, "This Tobo hath passed the Inspection of our new law, every hogshead was cased and viewed by which means the tobacco was very much tumbled and made something less sightly than it was before and it causes a great deal of extraordinary trouble". There were complaints that the new law destroyed tobacco that used to bring good money. Still another planter complained that the planter's name and evidence on the hogshead had much more effect on the price of the tobacco than the inspector's brand. While some of the planters expressed their disapproval of the new inspection law verbally, others resorted to violence. During the first year some villains burned two inspection houses, one in Lancaster County and another in Northumberland.

The inspection law passed in 1730 was frequently amended during the colonial period, but there were no changes in its essential features. The act provided that no tobacco was to be shipped except in hogsheads, cases, or casks, without having first passed an inspection at one of the legally established inspection warehouses; thus the shipment of bulk tobacco was prohibited. Two inspectors were employed at each warehouse, and a third was summoned in case of a dispute between the two regular inspectors. These officials were bonded and were forbidden under heavy penalties to pass bad tobacco, engage in the tobacco trade, or to take rewards. Tobacco offered in payment of debts, public or private, had to be inspected under the same conditions as that to be exported. The inspectors were required to open the hogshead, extract and carefully examine two samplings; all trash and unsound tobacco was to be burned in the warehouse kiln in the presence and with the consent of the owner. If the owner refused consent the entire hogshead was to be destroyed. After the tobacco was sorted, the good tobacco was repacked in the hogshead and the planter's distinguishing mark, net weight, tare (weight of the hogshead), and name of inspection warehouse were stamped on the hogshead.

A tobacco note was issued to the owner of each hogshead that passed the inspection. These notes were legal tender within the county issued, and adjacent counties, except when the counties were separated by a large river. They circulated freely and eventually came into the possession of a buyer who, by presenting them at the warehouse named on the notes, exchanged them for the specified amount of tobacco. And these particular notes were thus retired from circulation. The person finally demanding possession of the tobacco was allowed to have the hogsheads reinspected if he so desired. If he was dissatisfied with the quality, he could appeal to three justices of the peace. If they found the tobacco to be unsound or trashy, the inspectors paid a fee of five shillings to each of the justices, and they were also held liable for stamping the tobacco as being good; should the tobacco be declared sound, the buyer paid the fee.

Parcels of tobacco weighing less than 200 pounds in 1730, later increased to 350, and finally 950 pounds, were not to be exported, in such cases the inspectors issued transfer notes. When the purchaser of such tobacco had enough to fill a hogshead, the tobacco was prized and the transfer notes were exchanged for a tobacco note. The tobacco could then be exported. Such small parcels were often necessary to pay a levy, or a creditor, or it might have been tobacco left over from the crop after the last hogshead had been filled and prized. These tobacco notes provided the only currency in Virginia until she resorted to the printing press during the French and Indian War. By the end of the eighteenth century the reputation of the inspectors and the value of the tobacco notes began to decline, due primarily to lax inspecting. Exporters and manufacturers frequently demanded that their tobacco be reinspected by competent agents.

The inspection law was allowed to expire in October, 1775, but it was revived the following October. During this period the payment of debts in tobacco was made on the plantation of the debtor, and if the creditor refused to accept the tobacco as sound and marketable, the dispute was referred to two competent neighbors, one chosen by each of the disputants.

Prior to 1776 tobacco that was damaged while stored in the public warehouses was paid for by the colony, but provisions were made in 1776 that such a loss was to be borne by the owner of the tobacco. In 1778 this was amended to the effect that losses by fire while stored in the warehouses would be paid for by the state. Four years later, owing to the great losses that had been sustained by the owners of the tobacco, the inspectors were held liable for all tobacco destroyed or damaged, except by fire, flood, or the enemy. The state continued to guarantee the tobacco against the fire hazard until well into the nineteenth century.

The law requiring "refused" tobacco to be burned in the warehouse kiln was repealed in 1805, and such tobacco could then be shipped anywhere within the state of Virginia. Stemmers or manufacturers were required to send a certificate of receipt of such refused tobacco purchased to the auditor of public accounts in Richmond. These receipts were then checked against the warehouse records of the amount of refused tobacco sold. Finally, in 1826, the General Assembly legalized the exportation of refused tobacco, provided the word "refused" was stamped on both ends and two sides of the hogsheads in letters at least three inches in length.

In 1730 three inspectors were appointed for each inspection by the governor, with the advice and consent of the Council. This did not always mean that there were three inspectors at each warehouse at all times. Warehouses built on opposite banks of a creek or river were frequently placed under the same inspection; that is, the three inspectors divided their time at the two warehouses. In areas where the production of tobacco declined from time to time, two warehouses were frequently placed under the jurisdiction of one set of inspectors. And if the quantity of tobacco produced in that particular area necessitated separate inspections, the change was then made. The inspection system was very flexible in this respect. The inspectors were required to be on duty from October 1 to August 10 yearly, except Sundays and holidays. By 1732 it was discovered that it was unnecessary to have three inspectors on duty at all times. Consequently, the number of regular inspectors was reduced to two, but a third was appointed to be called upon when there was a dispute between the two regular inspectors as to the quality of tobacco.

As the governor was able to choose the inspectors and place them at any warehouse within the colony, the local county people began to complain and demand that they be given more authority in this governmental function. This procedure tended to provide the governor with the opportunity to provide his friends with jobs regardless of their qualifications. In 1738 the General Assembly enacted legislation providing that the inspectors were to be appointed by the governor from a slate of four candidates nominated by the local county courts. Where two warehouses under one inspection were in different counties, two candidates were to be nominated by each county. This procedure remained unchanged until the middle of the nineteenth century.

The salaries of the inspectors were regulated by the General Assembly, though the colony did not guarantee the sums after 1755. For the first few years each inspector received £60 annually, and if the fees collected were insufficient to pay their salary, the deficient amount was made up out of public funds. After 1732 it was found that this amount was too high and unequally allocated with respect to the amount of individual services performed, as some warehouses received more tobacco than others. So for the next few years salaries were determined on the basis of the amount of tobacco inspected and ranged from £30 to £50 annually. From 1755 to 1758 the inspectors received the amount set by the legislature only if enough fees were collected by the inspectors at their respective warehouses. During the next seven years the inspectors received three shillings per hogshead, plus six pence for nails used in recoopering the tobacco, instead of a stated salary. Out of this the inspectors had to pay the proprietors of the warehouse eight pence rent per hogshead. In 1765 the inspectors were again placed on a flat salary basis, and for the next fifteen years their salaries ranged from £25 to £70. After 1780 their annual salaries ranged from about $100 at the smallest warehouses to about $330 at the largest.

WAREHOUSES 1730-1800

In most instances the warehouses were private property, but they were always subject to the control of the legislature. Regulations regarding the location, erection, maintenance and operation as official places of inspection were set forth by special legislation. Owners of the land sites selected were ordered to build the warehouses and rent them to the inspectors. If the land owner refused to build, then the court could order the warehouse built at public expense. Just how many warehouses were built at public expense is difficult to determine, probably only a few, if any, were built in this manner.

The rent which the proprietor received usually depended upon the number of hogsheads inspected at his warehouse, though the rates were regulated by the General Assembly. In 1712 the proprietors received twelve pence for the first day or the first three months and six pence every month thereafter per hogshead. In 1755 the owners received eight pence per hogshead. During the Revolution the rate was raised to four shillings, but was lowered to one shilling six pence after the cessation of hostilities. At the beginning of the nineteenth century rent per hogshead, including a year's storage, was twenty-five cents.

To keep pace with the movement of the tobacco industry, new warehouses were built and others discontinued from time to time. And by observing the warehouse movement it is possible to grasp a general picture of the decline of the tobacco industry in Tidewater Virginia. The expansion of the industry into Piedmont is more difficult to follow during this period owing to the fact that inspection houses were not permitted above the Falls until after the Revolution.

In 1730 seventy-two warehouses located in thirty counties were ordered erected and maintained for the purpose of inspection and storage by the General Assembly. Twelve years later warehouses were erected in only one additional county, Fairfax. A few of those established in 1730 were discontinued, but twenty-six new ones had been erected by 1742, making a total of ninety-three in operation at that time. From 1742 to 1765 the total number of inspection houses increased by about six, but this does not reveal a complete picture of the warehouse movement. A closer examination shows a much greater shift in the movement. Sixteen new inspection warehouses were erected during this period, twelve of them near the Fall Line; in the meantime, ten of the old established warehouses far below the Falls were discontinued.

After a year without an official inspection system the lapsed inspection law was revived in October, 1776; seventy-six of the warehouses were re-established as official inspection stations. Soon after the end of the war the number of inspections began to increase again, and it was chiefly through the efforts of a David Ross that inspection warehouses were permitted above the Falls. The first inspections seem to have appeared above the Falls in Virginia in 1785: one at Crow's Ferry, Botetourt County; one at Lynch's Ferry, Campbell County; and a third at Point of Fork on the Rivanna River, Fluvanna County. Tobacco inspected in the warehouses above the Falls could not be legally delivered for exportation without first being delivered to a lower warehouse for transportation and reinspection upon demand by the purchaser.

There were a number of reasons why the inspection warehouses were restricted to Tidewater Virginia until after the Revolution. It was not until after the Revolution that a strong need and demand for them was felt above the Falls. Inadequate transportation facilities in the interior made exportation from upland inspections less feasible. It is also probable that the Legislature was opposed to upland inspections as it would be more difficult to control the inspections, spread out over a larger area, as rigidly as those concentrated in a smaller area. And no doubt Tidewater Virginia recognized the economic value of having all of the inspections located in its own section. However, the sharp decline in tobacco production in the Tidewater followed by an equal increase in the Piedmont made inspections above the Falls inevitable.

Of the ninety-three inspection warehouses in operation in 1792, only about twenty were above the Fall Line; but by 1820 at least half of the 137 legal inspections were above the Falls. Of the forty-two new inspections established in the period 1800-1820 only three were in Tidewater Virginia;

one in Prince George County in 1807, one in Essex County in 1810, and the third in Norfolk County in 1818, owing to the opening of the Dismal Swamp Canal.

SALE OF THE LEAF

Under the original plan of colonization the Virginia settlers were to pool their goods at the magazine, the general storehouse in Jamestown. All of the products produced by the settlers, and all goods imported into the colony were to be first brought to the magazine. In 1620 the London Company made plans to abolish the magazine and open the trade to the public. The colony was then forced to rely on peripatetic merchant ships which came irregularly. These casual traders dealt directly with the planters, going about from plantation to plantation collecting their cargo. These merchants were without agents in the colonies, and they relied solely upon the chance of selling their goods as they passed the various plantation wharves. They usually sold their goods on credit, expecting to collect their dues in tobacco on the return trip the next year. Occasionally the crops were small, or they discovered that most of the tobacco had been sold or seized by other traders, and consequently they were forced to wait another year to collect from their debtors.

The planter soon discovered that he was in an equally precarious situation, and largely at the mercy of the merchant, for if he failed to sell on the terms offered, another ship might not come his way until the following year. The planter's bargaining power was also hampered by his ignorance of market conditions abroad. Such conditions encouraged the practices of engrossing and forestalling, by the merchants, to the point that much legislation was passed to prohibit such actions. Increasing competition by the Dutch traders gradually reduced the dependence of the planter on the casual trading merchant. The danger from pirates and frequent wars caused the English to inaugurate the convoy system, which also helped improve the market conditions. However, trading directly with the casual merchants was still common after 1625, and a few still operated as late as 1700.

The consignment system developed along with the system of casual trading, and it also operated upon the practice of the ships collecting cargo from the various plantations. Importation was based on the same idea: the ship which gathered the planters' tobacco usually brought goods from abroad. Originally the merchant acted only as the agent of the planter. He advanced him the total cost necessary to export and market the crop abroad, sold the crop on his client's account and placed the net proceeds to the planter's credit. Soon the merchant was advancing the planter goods and money beyond the amount of his net receipts; the planter frequently discovered that he was at the merchant's mercy and was forced to sell on the merchant's terms. To make matters worse, the tobacco was sold by the merchants to retailers in England on long term credit at the planter's risk. If the retailer went bankrupt, or his business failed, the planter not only lost his tobacco but still had to pay the total charges, freight, insurance, British duties, plus the agent's commission, which amounted to about eighteen pounds sterling in 1730. Planters frequently complained that their tobacco weighed much less in England that it did when it was inspected and weighed in the colony. There were reports that the stevedores were supplying certain patrons in England with tobacco of superior quality obtained by pilfering. An agent in England was certainly not apt to look after a planter's crop as though it were his own.

The gradual destruction of the fertility of the soil in the Tidewater country and the expansion of the tobacco industry into the back country made direct consignment less feasible. This, and the various other causes of dissatisfaction with the consignment system, led to the system of outright purchase in the colony. This new procedure was carried on largely by the outport merchants, especially the Scottish, who were doing quite a bit of illicit trading before the Union of 1707. Since the Tidewater business was controlled largely by the London merchants, the new Scottish traders penetrated the interior and established local trading posts or stores at convenient locations, many of which became the nuclei of towns. After the Union their share of the trade increased very rapidly, and at the beginning of hostilities in 1775 the Scots were purchasing almost one-half of all the tobacco brought to Great Britain. On the eve of the Revolution only about one-fourth of the Virginia tobacco was being shipped on consignment.

The factorage system appears to have been introduced in Virginia around 1625, and was actually a part of the consignment system. A factor was one who resided in the colony and served as a representative and the repository of the English merchant. With the establishment of a repository in the colony, trade became more regular, debtors less delinquent, and the problem of securing transportation for exports or imports was mitigated. Some of the factors were Englishmen sent over by the English firms, others were colonial merchants or planters who performed for the foreign firms on a commission basis. As the tobacco industry expanded beyond the limits of the navigable waters, it became the custom of the planters located near such streams to act as factors for their neighbors in the interior. By 1775 the factorage system had developed to the extent that one planter found four firms at Colchester, eleven at Dumfries, and twenty at Alexandria which would buy wheat, tobacco, and flour in exchange for British goods and northern manufactures.

The rise of a class of factors in Virginia, aided by the Scottish merchants, made it possible for the planters to break away from the London commercial agents. The Revolution cut the connection between England and the Virginia planters, but the factorage system was not destroyed. The merchants and businessmen in the former colonies simply replaced the English factors. Soon after the cessation of hostilities, England had reestablished her commercial predominance owing to the superior facilities and experience of British merchants in granting long term credits, and perhaps the preference of Americans for British goods. The British were again willing to extend to the planters the accustomed long term credits, but they were careful to grant it only to merchants of high standing.

Lax inspecting caused the buyers to lose faith in the inspectors' reputation and guarantee. As early as 1759 tobacco was being sold by displaying samples. It was quite natural then for the buyers to begin visiting the warehouses as the tobacco was being inspected, to enable them to purchase the better hogsheads directly from the original owner. But it seems that even as late as 1800 such practices were only occasional. While lax inspections caused a few buyers to visit the warehouses, the presence of these buyers led many of the planters to bring their tobacco to the warehouses most frequented by the buyers. As these buyers paid higher prices for the better tobacco, the ultimate result was the development of market towns and the disappearance of the tobacco note. Within a decade after the turn of the nineteenth century Richmond, Manchester, Petersburg, and Lynchburg had become major market towns.

PRODUCTION, TREND OF PRICES, AND EXPORTS

When tobacco was first planted in Jamestown, Spanish tobacco was selling for eighteen shillings per pound. Virginia tobacco was inferior in quality, but it was assessed in England at ten shillings per pound. On the basis of these high prices the Virginia Company of London agreed to allow the Virginia planters three shillings per pound, in trade at the magazine in Jamestown, for the best grades.

Even though it seemed that the London Company was getting the lions share, these prices proved to be very profitable for the colonists and the infant tobacco industry increased very rapidly. During the period 1615-1622 tobacco exports increased from 2,300 to 60,000 pounds, and by 1630 the volume had risen to 1,500,000. Meanwhile prices had fallen as rapidly as production and exports had increased. In 1625 tobacco was selling for about two shillings per pound, but in 1630 merchants were reported to be buying it for less than one penny per pound.

It was quite obvious that the fall in prices was due to overproduction. The English first attempted to alleviate the condition in 1619 through monopolistic control. Negotiations were conducted with the Virginia Company of London, Henry Somerscales, and Ditchfield in 1625. All were opposed by the colony, except that of the London Company, because the colonists thought that the various proposals would benefit the King and a small group of court favorites at the expense of the planters.

The next move was made by the colony. In an attempt to restrict the production of tobacco, Governor Wyatt ordered that production be limited to 1,000 plants per person in each family in 1621. These same instructions provided that only nine leaves were to be harvested from each plant. Similar laws were enacted in 1622 and again in 1629, but these laws were probably not strictly enforced as prices failed to improve. Undaunted by failure in its first attempt to cope with the situation, the General Assembly made several attempts at price fixing. In 1632 tobacco prices in the colony were fixed at six pence per pound in exchange for English goods; in 1633 it was increased to nine pence.

The 1639 crop was so large that the legislature ordered all of the bad and half of the good tobacco destroyed; merchants were required to accept fifty pounds of tobacco per 100 of indebtedness. English goods were to be exchanged for tobacco at a minimum rate of three pence per pound. The minimum rate of the 1640 crop was fixed at twelve pence. Such legislation failed to meet with the approval of the home government and in 1641 tobacco averaged about two pence per pound.

Following the depression of 1639 tobacco prices failed to rise above three pence, and probably never averaged more than two pence per pound for the next sixty years. To prevent the complete ruination of the tobacco planters, the General Assembly established fixed rates for tobacco in the payment of certain fees. In 1645 these fees were payable in tobacco rated at one and one-half pence per pound; ten years later the rate had increased only a half pence. The war with Holland, restrictions on the Dutch trade, and the plague in England brought forth another serious depression in the colonies in the 1660's. In 1665 the tobacco fleet did not go to the colonies on account of the plague in London. Tobacco prices dropped to one pence per pound.

METHODS OF TRANSPORTING TOBACCO TO MARKET
a, Upon canoes. b, By upland boats. c, By wagons. d, Rolling the hogshead.

**PLANTATION TOBACCO HOUSES AND PUBLIC
WAREHOUSES**
a, The common tobacco house. b, Tobacco hanging on a scaffold. c,
The operation of prizing. d, Inside of a tobacco house, showing the
tobacco hanging to cure. e, An outside view of a public warehouse. f,
showing the process of Inspection.

This new depression stirred the Virginia legislature. In 1662 the Assembly
prohibited the planting of tobacco after the last of June, provided that

Maryland would do the same. Maryland rejected the idea. This would have eliminated a great deal of inferior tobacco, for much of the tobacco planted in July seldom fully matures before it must be harvested to save it from the frost. The planters in both colonies continued to produce excessive crops and the depression became more acute. Led by Virginia, the North Carolina and Maryland legislatures prohibited the cultivation of tobacco in 1666. Lord Baltimore again refused to permit a cessation in Maryland, consequently Virginia and North Carolina repealed their legislation. Instead of cessation the Virginia crop was so large in 1666 that 100 vessels were not enough to export the crop. The possibility of another enormous crop in 1667 was eliminated by a severe storm that destroyed two-thirds of the crop. However, the glutted market resulting from the large crop grown in 1666 caused prices to fall to a half pence per pound.

In the 1670's prices climbed to one and one-half pence, but a tremendous crop in 1680 glutted the market again. The crop was said to have been so large that it would have supplied the demand for the next two years, even if none were produced in 1681. The General Assembly once again came to the aid of the planter by rating tobacco in payment of debts at one and one-fifth pence in 1682, and two pence in payment of quit-rents in 1683. Once again Virginia renewed attempts to bring about a cessation of production, but the English government refused to permit such action claiming that it would stimulate foreign production and thereby reduce the revenue to the Crown. In April, 1682 the General Assembly convened but was prorogued by Lieutenant Governor Sir Henry Chicheley a week later, when it was apparent that the members were determined to discuss nothing but the cessation of tobacco. A week later a series of plant cuttings broke out in Gloucester County followed by others in New Kent and Middlesex counties. Approximately 10,000 hogsheads of tobacco were destroyed before these riots were put down by the militia. Probably as a result of this destructive act, prices rose to two and a half pence in 1685, but a bumper crop of over 18,000,000 pounds in 1688, the largest ever produced to that date, caused prices to drop to one penny per pound in 1690.

Throughout most of the seventeenth century the tobacco planters were plagued with the problem of overproduction and low prices. To add to their woes the entire eighteenth century was one of periodic wars either in Europe or in America, or both. King William's War ended in 1697 and the following year tobacco prices soared to twenty shillings per hundred pounds and prices remained good for the next few years. The outbreak of Queen Anne's War and another 18,000,000 pound crop ushered in another depression. Several thousand hogsheads of tobacco shipped on consignment in 1704 brought no return at all, and the next year many of the planters sold their tobacco for one-fourth of a penny per pound. Instead of attempting to limit production in an effort to relieve the market conditions, these low prices caused the planters to increase production as they attempted to meet their obligations. In 1709 tobacco production reached an all-time high of 29,000,000 pounds.

The Peace of Utrecht in 1713 seems to have brought little relief. Tobacco prices failed to improve until after the passage of the inspection act in 1730. In 1731 tobacco sold for as much as twelve shillings six pence per hundred pounds, despite the fact that Virginia exported 34,000,000 pounds. In a further attempt to improve the quality and the price of tobacco the General Assembly ordered the constables in each district to enforce the law forbidding the planters to harvest suckers. Anyone found tending suckers after the last of July was to be heavily penalized. These two measures seem to have produced the desired effects; in 1736 tobacco sold for fifteen shillings per hundred pounds.

Unlike Queen Anne's War, King George's War seemed to stimulate tobacco prices and they remained relatively good for a number of years after the Peace of Aix-la-Chapelle in 1748. During the early 1750's merchants paid up to twenty shillings per hundred pounds, even though Virginia had been exporting from 38,000,000 to 53,000,000 pounds annually. During the French and Indian War the belligerents agreed to continue the tobacco trade, but in spite of this arrangement there were unusual price fluctuations owing primarily to inflation and occasional poor crops. In 1755 a period of inflation was created when Virginia resorted to the printing press for currency. At the same time war operations hampered production and only about one-half of the usual annual crop was produced, and tobacco prices rose to twenty shillings per hundred weight. During the years of peace just prior to the American Revolution, tobacco averaged about three pence per pound and never fell below two pence. With the outbreak of hostilities the General Assembly prohibited the exportation of tobacco to the British Empire.

Frequent overproduction and the numerous wars during the eighteenth century seem to have caused more violent price fluctuations than those of the previous century. Although the American colonies did not participate in all of the wars involving England, all of them had their effects upon the colonies. Virginia depended primarily upon England to transport her tobacco crop and during the war years there was a frequent shortage of ships used for the tobacco trade. As this cut off the tobacco supply to the foreign markets, many of them began to grow their supply of tobacco.

The tobacco crops were small almost every year during the Revolution. Owing to the increase in the demand for foodstuffs many of the planters switched from tobacco to wheat. During the first year of the war tobacco exports dropped from 55,000,000 to 14,500,000 pounds. It has been said that for the entire period 1776-1782 Virginia's exports were less than her exports of a single year before the Revolution. Wartime prices and inflation caused tobacco prices to increase from eighteen shillings per hundred pounds in 1775 to 2,000 shillings, in Continental currency, in 1781. An official account in the latter part of 1780 related that twenty-five shillings per hundred pounds in specie was considered a very substantial price. A very small crop in 1782 was followed by one that topped any of the pre-war crops, and by 1787 prices had fallen to fifteen pence per pound. Prices dropped to $12.00 in 1791, and a period of relatively low prices continued until 1797 when prices increased as a result of an extensive shift from tobacco to wheat. In 1800 prices dropped to $7.40 per hundred pounds as Virginia exported a near record crop of over 78,000 hogsheads of tobacco.

VIRGINIA TOBACCO PRICES AND EXPORTS, 1615-1789

A complete and accurate price table would be virtually impossible to compile. Some of these averages represent only single individual quotations, or the average of only two or three such quotations. These charts are intended to give the reader a general picture of the prices during the Colonial period.

Year	Average Price per Lb.		Average Price per Cwt.	Pounds Exported
1615	3s			2,300
1617	3s			20,000
1618	3s			41,000
1619	3s			44,879
1620	2s	6d		40,000
1621	3s			55,000
1622	3s			60,000
1623	2s			
1625	2s	4d		
1626	3s			500,000
1628	3s	6d		500,000
1629	3s			1,500,000

1630	1d	1,500,000
1631	6d	1,300,000
1632	6d	
1633	9d	
1634	1d	
1637	9d	
1638	2d	
1639	3d	1,500,000
1640	12d	1,300,000
1641	2d	1,300,000
1642	2d	
1644	1-1/2d	
1645	1-1/2d	
1649	3d	
1651	16s	
1652	20s	
1655	2d	
1656	2d	
1657	3d	
1658	2d	
1659	2d	
1660	2d	
1661	2d	
1662	2d	
1664	1-1/2d	

1665	1d		
1666	1-1/5d		
1667	1/2d		
1669		20s	
1676	1-1/2d		
1682	1-1/5d		
1683	2d		
1684	1/2d		
1685	2-1/2d		
1686	1-1/5d		
1688			18,295,000
1690	1d		
1691	2d		
1692	1d		
1695	1-1/2d		
1696	1-1/5d		
1697	1/2d		22,000,000
1698		20s	22,000,000
1699		20s	22,000,000
1700		10s	average
1701			average
1702		20s	
1704	2d		18,000,000
1706	1/4d		
1709	1d		29,000,000

1710	1d		
1713		3s	
1715		2s	
1716		11s	
1720	1d		
1722	3/4d		
1723	1d		
1724	1-1/2d		
1727	9d		
1729	10d		
1731		12s 6d	34,000,000
1732	9d		34,000,000
1733	2d		34,000,000
1736	2d		34,000,000
1737	9d		average
1738	3d		average
1739	2d		average
1740			34,000,000
1744	2d		47,000,000
1745		14s	38,232,900
1746	2d		36,217,800
1747			37,623,600
1748		16s 8d	42,101,700
1749	2d		43,880,300
1750		15s	43,710,300

1751			16s	43,032,700
1752		2d		43,542,000
1753			20s	53,862,300
1754				45,722,700
1755		2d		42,918,300
1756			20s	25,606,800
1757		3d		
1758		3d		22,050,000
1759			35s	55,000,000
1760				55,000,000
1761			22s 6d	55,000,000
1762		11d		55,000,000
1763		2d		55,000,000
1764			12s 6d	55,000,000
1765		3d		55,000,000
1766	4s			average
1767	3s	10d		average
1768			22s 6d	average
1769			23s	average
1770			25s	average
1771			18s	average
1772			20s	average
1773			12s 6d	average
1774			13s	average
1775		3-1/4d		55,000,000

1776		12s	14,498,500
1777		34s	12,441,214
1778		70s	11,961,333
1779		400s	17,155,907
1780		1,000s	17,424,967
1781		2,000s	13,339,168
1782		36s	9,828,244
1783		40s	86,649,333
1784		30s 10d	49,497,000
1785		30s	55,624,000
1786	19d		60,380,000
1787	15d		60,041,000
1788		25s	58,544,000
1789	15d		58,673,000

CONCLUSION

The history of tobacco is the history of Jamestown and of Virginia. No one staple or resource ever played a more significant role in the history of any state or nation. The growth of the Virginia Colony, as it extended beyond the limits of Jamestown, was governed and hastened by the quest for additional virgin soil in which to grow this "golden weed." For years the extension into the interior meant the expansion of tobacco production. Without tobacco the development of Virginia might have been retarded 200 years.

Tobacco was the life and soul of the colony; yet a primitive, but significant, form of diversified farming existed from the very beginning especially among the small farmers. Even with the development of the large plantations in the eighteenth century, there were quite a number of small landowners interspersed among the big planters in the Tidewater area, and they were most numerous in the Piedmont section. They usually possessed few slaves, if any, and raised mostly grains, vegetables and stock which they could easily sell to neighboring tobacco planters. The negligible food imports by the colony indicates that a regular system of farming existed. Nor was tobacco the sole product of the large tobacco plantations. This is indicated by the fact that practically all of the accounts of the product of one man's labor were recorded as so many pounds or acres of tobacco plus provisions. And had the plantations not been generally self-sufficient, the frequently extremely low prevailing tobacco prices would have made the agricultural economy even less profitable.

Tobacco was a completely new agricultural product to most, if not all, of the English settlers at Jamestown. There were no centuries of vast experience in growing, curing, and marketing to draw upon. These problems and procedures were worked out by trial and error in the wilderness of Virginia. Tobacco became the only dependable export and the colony was exploited for the benefit of English commerce. This English commercial policy, plus other factors, caused the Virginia planter to become somewhat of an agricultural spendthrift. For nearly 200 years he followed a system of farming which soon exhausted his land. Land was cheap and means of fertilization was limited and laborious. By clearing away the trees he was able to move north, south, southwest, and west and replace his worn-out fields with rich virgin soil necessary to grow the best tobacco.

While struggling with the problems involved in producing an entirely new crop about which they knew little or nothing, the colonists also had to feed themselves, deal with their racial problems, and maintain a stable local government as they continually expanded in a limitless wilderness. Out of all this chaos grew the mother and leader of the American colonies.

Tobacco penetrated the social, political, and economic life of the colony. Ownership of a large tobacco plantation could take one up the social ladder; many of the men responsible for the welfare of the colony were planters, and everything could be paid for in tobacco. In 1620 the indentured servants were paid for with tobacco, the young women sent to the colonists to become wives were purchased by paying their transportation charges with tobacco. The wages of soldiers and the salaries of clergymen and governmental officials were paid in tobacco. After 1730 tobacco notes, that is warehouse receipts, representing a certain amount of money, served as currency for the colony.

The development of the inspection system with its chain of tobacco warehouses hastened urbanization. Around many of these warehouses grew villages and settlements; some of these eventually became towns and cities. Richmond, Petersburg, Danville, Fredericksburg, Farmville, Clarksville and others were once merely convenient landings or locations for tobacco warehouses. Even today the fragrant aroma of cured tobacco still exists in a number of these places during the tobacco marketing season. The tobacco trade was largely responsible for the birth and growth of Alexandria, Dumfries, and Norfolk into important export-import centers. For her birth, growth, and colonial leadership, Virginia pays her respect to John Rolfe and the other brave settlers at Jamestown.

Tobacco is still a vital factor in Virginia's economy. Of approximately 2,000,000 acres of cropland (pastureland excluded) in 1949, 115,400 were planted in tobacco which produced 124,904,000 pounds valued at $55,120,800 or twenty-three percent of the total value of all agricultural crops. Of the four largest agricultural products—poultry, tobacco, meat animals, and milk—tobacco ranked second only to poultry in terms of income in 1955. Poultry produced an income of $99,935,000, tobacco $84,128,000, meat animals $80,564,000, and milk $70,681,000. Peanuts and fruits were tied for fifth place, each producing an income of about $21,000,000.

Of the many different industries in Virginia today only five—food, textile, wearing apparel, chemical, and the manufacture of transportation equipment—employ more workers than the tobacco manufacturers. In 1953 a total of $40,000,000, in salaries and wages, was paid to production workers in the tobacco manufacturing industry in Virginia.

Although tobacco is no longer "king" in the Old Dominion, Virginia farmers produce enough of the "golden weed" each year to make one long cigarette that would stretch around the world fifty times.